Chapters:

12. Run a tight ship, but don't own the ship - It's God's team, not yours.

13. Be friends with everyone- but ASSOCIATE with the strong!

14. Characteristics of a healthy worshipper. (Characteristics of a Great Leader)

15. No more DRAMA!

16. Views on Secular Music

17. Five Basic Principles

18. Do songs from YOUR church!

19. Show me a sincere worshipper...and I'll show you a HUMBLE SERVANT.

20. HOW TO MAKE – Opening Videos

21. HOW TO MAKE – Transition Videos

22. Early is ON TIME – On time is LATE

23. SERVING is the greatest form of worship. (Serve your Pastor and his flock). Serve his vision and not yours. God will honor you for following the man that he has placed you under.

24. Never say NO!

25. Sorry – you don't have the best Pastor, WE DO

It is such an honor to bring you this teaching. I was sincerely humbled when asked to share the ideas and approaches that the Lord has laid upon my heart. I have had the privilege of putting these teachings into practice, through serving with Pastor Matthew Barnett for the past ten years here at Angelus Temple and the Dream Center.

The following chapters are for you, each Pastor, Youth Pastor and Worship Leader. It is my goal and intentions that you can find ideas and teachings that you can practically use to train and strengthen your church, your youth groups and most of all – the hearts of your worshippers.

The Foursquare Youth has committed themselves to equip, resource and inspire you, your staff members and your worship teams. Our focused and common goal is to build community, build leaders and build a bond of passionate worshippers that will revolutionize our movement and our nation for the Lord. I have seen and know the desire and passion that James Craft and Armando Alvarado have, to see you equipped with every resource – so that – you can impact your church and your community for Christ.

How blessed we are as a movement to have a President whose heart and life is centered and devoted to worship. How honored and humbled we are to serve under one of the greatest worship leaders and writers, as Pastor and President Jack Hayford.

In all actuality, the ideas and teachings you are about to read are a result and reflection of what I have learned through leading worship and serving under Pastors Matthew and Tommy Barnett. These teachings are a result of them training and pouring in to my life. For a total of 15 years, I have been able to sit under such incredible leaders. The first five years was as a lay- worship leader in Phoenix, AZ, with Pastor Tommy Barnett.

It was just over ten years ago when Pastor Tommy Barnett asked me to fly over to Los Angeles from Phoenix, to help look for a worship leader or music person to raise up at the Dream Center. Pastor Matthew had been in Los Angeles a couple of years at the time and was in need of a "Music Guy". Well little did I know that God was training me for that! I thought I was going to find someone to do it and then I could just fly back to comfortable and beautiful Phoenix. I think it was a surprise to Pastor Matthew too!

To make a long story short – I ended up doing the Sunday morning "First" service in Phoenix at 8:30 am and then flew to Los Angeles to do the 11:00 am service. Then flew back to Phoenix to be there Sunday night and Wednesday night – then flew back to Los Angeles to do the Thursday's services. I ended up doing that for one and a half years before the Lord called us here for good! We had the privilege of selling our house and belongings in Phoenix and we moved into one of the old hospital rooms at the Dream Center! Joined by my wonderful wife Gina, incredibly gifted daughter Tisha and my younger sister Kim – the Hanleys were about to find out the true meaning of worship!

The rest is history as they say – but I pray that you will find this book to be extremely motivating and very practical. There is nothing too big or small to prevent you and your church from exploding in passion and in numbers; and for it to come from a servant's heart for true worship. In other words – if the Lord can take me and the unusual and crazy things he had to work with here; and make what I believe is the most beautiful act of worship – trust me, he can do even greater things through you.

Pastor David Hanley
Press Play
Director of Music/ Worship
Angelus Temple/ The Dream Center

CHAPTER 1

"What is TRUE worship?"

I believe that this may be the questions of all questions and that this question is in the heart and mind of every worshipper. This question can be either the biggest motivator; or it can be the biggest unobtainable hurdle in our relationship with the Lord and the congregation that he has called us to.

I believe that before we can go any further in the "How To's" of worship, we must first have a clear and real understanding of just what "Worship" is. If you're like me, being raised all my life in ministry and in the church – I have inherently adopted other's preconceived ideas of what worship is or what they think it is supposed to be; instead of finding out what is the Lord's idea of worship.

Now of course, you are and should be asking yourself right now – what makes him the authority or why is his opinion the "Right" opinion. Congratulations! You've got it! You see, I believe that's just it! I encourage you to never be trapped or in bondage to anyone else's opinion or idea of what true worship is. The relationship that only you have with your creator, one on one, is unique and there is nothing and no one that can tell you how it ought to be. True worship is what you have going on with the Lord, Jesus Christ.

If you are a worship leader or director of music for a church, then you have a natural and spiritual obligation to wholeheartedly follow the direction and vision of the Pastor that the Lord has placed you under. There should be a sincere and non-manufactured loyalty to him and his vision. Your idea of worship should align with his as you faithfully serve the Lord, by serving your Pastor. Your Pastor that you serve under is expected to pour into your life by giving you direction and vision for the type and style of worship that the Lord has put in his heart as it pertains to the congregation. You see, your Pastor is responsible for the congregation and the Lord has placed him as the pulse detector of his flock. All you have to do is relax and follow his direction as unto the Lord.

If someone other than your Pastor is telling you or critiquing you or your worship – relax, they already are out of touch of what true worship is. Just pray for them because true worship is the farthest thing from a critiquing, critical and negative spirit. I have been in worship ministry for over 15 years and there has always been and always will be the critical people that really sincerely think they have the handle on what true worship is – but they are just the ones who really don't. I can't even tell you what your worship is unto the Lord. The relationship that you have with him is yours and not mine to critique.

Should worship be 30 minutes, instead of 20? Should it be spontaneous, or planned? Should it matter what it looks like? Sounds like? I believe too many people and churches have gotten caught up in all these things and have in fact turned away from the responsibilities of leadership and traded it in for what they think of is a MORE spiritual approach.

Liberate yourself in knowing that there are many different styles of churches and many different styles of worship – but they're just that, STYLES. This book is designed to help you really take yourself to the (oops another cliché) "Next Level." Honestly though, there is that next level and it can only be found in Christ and not in others. I will be the first to admit that I have been guilty of critiquing worship, critiquing the heart of the worshippers and forming my own narrow opinion of what I wanted worship to be – instead of just finding the heart of God.

I was a stubborn and slow learner but I hope the next few chapters can help you find and put into practice the life changing and very practical steps that helped me find my place in nothing else but the Lord.

It's all about your HEART!

Teaching and Scripture Reference:

Isaiah 29:13
Wherefore the Lord said, Forasmuch as this people draw near me with their mouth and with their lips do honor me; but have removed their heart far from me and their fear toward me is taught by the precept of men.

Mark 7: 6-7
He answered and said unto them, Well hath Esalas prophesied of you hypocrites, as it is written, this people honoureth me with their lips but their heart is far from me. Howbeit in vain do they worship me, teaching for the doctrines the commandments of men.

John 4:23-24
23 But the time is coming and is already here when true worshipers will worship the Father in spirit and in truth. The Father is looking for anyone who will worship him that way. 24 For God is Spirit, so those who worship him must worship in spirit and in truth."

1 Chronicles 22:19
Now set your heart and your soul to seek the LORD your God

TO SUM IT UP ...

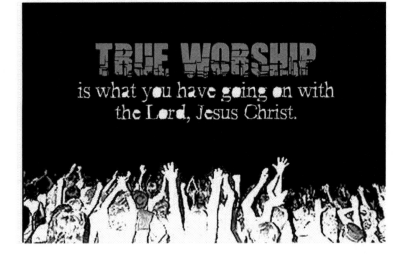

NOTES TO SELF...

The 4(FOUR) "E"s of WORSHIP

This is without a doubt one of the easiest and most practical things to teach and share with your team. Once you teach this to them – it will forever be referred to and they will latch onto it really quick.

These Four "E"s are what I use as the foundation and purpose behind everything we do. Every point and following sub-points are directed to each individual worship team member. Each point is designed to build a specific type of character in each worshipper; the kind we want serving along side of us. Each point is targeted at every worshipper and designed to motivate them to always have a clear understanding of their role and purpose, within the team and our church. I encourage you to do as we have and once you have completed your teaching of this – post it around your prayer room or wherever you frequently go as a team. This will always be a unifying and purpose declaring, mission statement. Challenge your team to posses these attributes:

HERE WE GO!

EXCELLENCE:

- <u>Excellence</u> in character – be an example to not only the congregation but to the worship team. Character is you prayer life, staying in the word....BE ON TIME! Be the example!

- <u>Excellence</u> in our gifting and talents – work hard and practice hard at what the Lord has given you to do. The world shows excellence with their God given talents – they're just not using them for God though. How much more should we be using and perfecting our skills to the fullest. Tight services, tight transitions, flawless videos and excellent planning.
- <u>Excellence</u> in attitude – Stay positive! Negative thinking and speaking will always empower your problem and keep you from your God made destiny. A negative, gossiping or jealous person is always the farthest thing from a worshipper. A worshipper of Christ is continually grateful and always is praising others.

ENTHUSIASM:

- <u>Enthusiasm</u> for souls – Soul winning, Soul winning! That will always be the heart beat of our team and church. Let your talent and your worship not be just about how you sound or jump – let your worship be judged by how many people's life will be changed because of your existence. Always keep your hearts broken for the lost. Be more excited and passionate for souls than any worship service or song.
- <u>Enthusiasm</u> for worship – yes we are a church and a team that are extremely excited about the extreme things God has done in all our lives. I want your excitement and appreciation to be evident. I want people to know, before they hear you, that you are excited about your God and you are excited to take them to him! You may never be heard audibly but your spirit needs to leap off that stage and into their souls, to help pull them and their attention toward Christ.
- <u>Enthusiasm</u> for other's successes and root them on! Be your teammate's biggest fans and prayer partners. Remember, with us we have over 60 people on the team but only 15 on the stage at any given service. However, the other 45 rotating

people are required to be in attendance at church (It's not a day off), they must sit in the first three rows, worship down front with the crowd and be in the altars praying for people.

EXPANSION:

- Expansion of your personal and spiritual relationship w/ the Lord. There should be signs of constant spiritual growth and maturity.
- Ever expanding the team, songs, visuals – this is evidence of time with God! Keep the team ever growing. The Pastors and congregation should always be able to count on the worship team being as strong in numbers and quality from one week to the next. Each week should be better than the last and never let there be a down week. Let everyone in your church use the strength and consistency of your worship team, as a drawing card to get people through the doors. Let them count on it to always be great!
- Expand your compassion and your grace. Ask the Lord to continually expand your heart for people – and he will! Worshippers should always be increasing in the giving of grace to others.
- Expand your involvement in outreach and church ministries. I recommend to not keep the team just involved in music. Encourage them to be involved in many ministries. This actually gives credibility to their worship with their fellow peers.
- Expand your giving of tithes and offerings!!! And every Pastor said? Amen! The worshipper's heart is an example of a grateful and generous heart – therefore it must be evident through giving!

EVANGELISTIC:

- Evangelism within the team – pray for one another, love one another and serve one another. You know how important I feel being involved in outreach is – but you must also serve and love the people that the Lord has called you to minister with.

- <u>Evangelism</u> through outreach – stay in the "Uncomfortable Zone". Make yourself be in some type of outreach – BE AT ADOPT-A-BLOCK!
- <u>Evangelism</u> as worship – you've heard me say several times throughout these chapters in several different manners but the message is very clear. The worship team's mission is clear – we are there to prepare the ground so that Pastor may plant the word and yield a harvest. In other words – we want to capture the congregation's attention as soon as they walk through the doors – we then want to direct their attention vertical, to Jesus Christ – to open up their minds to more than what they were thinking – so that, Pastor Matthew can plant the word of the Lord to fertile soil – HERE'S THE PAY OFF! - so that, when the altar call is given….there is nothing stopping them from coming to the front and accepting Jesus Christ as their Savior!
- <u>Remember</u>, there's no way to live for Jesus – without living for others!

Teaching and Scripture Reference:

(Enthusiasm)
2 Corinthians 9:1-2
9:1 There is no need for me to write to you about this service to the saints. 2 For I know your eagerness to help, and I have been boasting about it to the Macedonians, telling them that since last year you in Achaia were ready to give; and your enthusiasm has stirred most of them to action.

I THESSALONIANS 5:16
Rejoice in the Lord always and I again I say rejoice!

(Excellence)
I CORINTHIANS 10:31
Whatever you do, do it all for the Glory of God

ECCLESIASTES 9:10
Whatsoever thy hand findeth to do, do it with thy might

(Expansion) EX.PAN.SION
Websters dictionary: enlargement,
Step-up, increase-the act of increasing something

2 Peter 1:5
for if you possess these qualities in increasing measure,
they will keep you from being ineffective in your knowledge
of our LORD

(Evangelistic)euaggelistes"a bringer of good
news"

MARK 16:15
And then he told them, "Go into all the world and preach
the Good News to everyone, everywhere.

TO SUM IT UP ...

NOTES TO SELF...

"One God, one Pastor, one Vision – one TEAM"

This is the most revolutionary, church advancing and team improvement things I've ever done or seen! If you could only teach or take one thing from this book – take this one! Do this – it can be made to fit any Pastor, church and team. Formulate this plan to fit your church and team – but don't give yourself one excuse not to do it. You'll forever love it – but your Pastor and congregation will love it even more!

On any given service at Angelus Temple/ The Dream Center – you will always see the same amount of people on the platform. Currently, there are a total of 15 people including band, vocals and myself. However, Press Play (the music team of Angelus Temple and the Dream Center) has over 60 people on the team and growing every week. Here's how –

Each position of the entire team (TEAM –remember who I define the TEAM as being), has 3-5 people for that position. In other words – we rotate every position with 3 – 5 other qualified people, every service. Even I, myself rotates every week!

There are so many benefits and reasons we do this and here are just a few:

- I first saw and experienced Darlene Zschech doing this approach with Hillsong. I then formulated and expanded it to fit the needs of our church and Pastor Matthew's needs and vision.

- Once a month, my wife and I sit down and write out a complete schedule for the entire month. This schedule contains the players, vocals and worship leaders for the next month – BUT GET THIS – this schedule is for the whole church. All players, vocals , etc – for every ministry of the church. Not just the main services but depending on what season of ministry that our church is in; we are one team covering all ages and departments of our church. From the little grade school kids in Kids Church to the Seniors, or even for the Healing Services – our team, one team, one vision is carrying a consistent and unified thread throughout the entire church. Have you ever experienced a church where the youth, singles or even Master's Commission would really worship the Lord passionately in their own services but then they wouldn't seem like the same people in the main services? Well this is not true at Angelus Temple and the Dream Center. Our congregation has learned that God doesn't change regardless of which room they're standing in; and neither does their heart for God.

- I don't think any churches or their staff has ever intentionally created clicks within their own congregation but it is a very simple thing to accidentally create. I believe that we must create services and ministries that will attract, mentor and appeal to all age groups and sectors. However, I believe we must always keep a strong thread of unity and vision from our senior Pastor. Some churches have accidentally created various services throughout the week for various age groups that actually alienate those same people when it comes to the main services on Sunday.

Pastor Matthew refers to every Sunday Service as "The Super Bowl"; so therefore we have the same members of the worship team already relating and making relationships throughout the entire week. That way, regardless of the age of these groups and other departments; when we all come together for the main services- everybody already has been worshipping together all week. There's no US vs THEM mentality.

- It's one team regardless of what service we're in. It's one team rooting each other on. It's one team cheering on the other players and singers when they do a solo! That's right – nobody owns a solo! The sound of our team is consistent. Regardless of whose in what given position for that service – our sound doesn't change. I believe this is important. Consistency is something that your Pastors and congregation should be able to count on. If you go to a U2 or Coldplay concert, they are going to have their signature sound. They have figured out that regardless of who may be substituting on the drums, their fans can count on it sounding like U2. You can read more on this topic in the 4 "E's" (Excellence) chapter in this book.

- This will provide you, your team, your Pastor and your church with unlimited people and resources to better serve your church. Open up the doors for everybody to be involved! I think choirs are great but you don't need a choir to have a huge music department. The music department should attract people from your community, to your church. The rotation concept allows you to continually grow in numbers even if you don't have a big stage to put them on.

- This will teach and train your worshippers to give their time and talent unto the Lord through serving the church. This will teach them to not be territorial with their worship. (Read my chapter on "Search for the HEART – not the Talent). No one owns any solos or positions. Even I rotate every week. (Read my chapter on "Run a tight ship – but don't own the ship")

- Your Pastor and your congregation will always look forward to and get a kick out of seeing new faces on the platform.

- Everybody on your team feels apart of something great and bigger than themselves. Everybody is encouraged to be part of the vision and creativity process of the worship and the church.

- There is strength in numbers! Having a team full of rotating people whose hearts are there for the right reasons – helps either develop and/or extinguish bad attitudes or incoming pre-madonnas. Be honest – you have them too! The cool thing about having a team of right hearts is that the pre-madonnas don't stand a chance. They either catch the servant-ship mentality really quick or they last about a day and find their way to be blessings at your churches! ☺

- When any given team member is rotating off or in other words, is not on the platform for that service – it is not a day off for them. They must be in attendance at church, seated in the first three rows, cheering on and praying for the team and Pastor Matthew and in the altars. Remember the other chapters, for all of us to have the honor of being able to be a part of this worship team and serving our church, Pastor and the Lord – we must be involved in the ministry of outreach to hurting people.

- My heart and the vision of this team will always be for our local church. The Lord is blessing our church and the vision to grow Angelus Temple and complete the construction of the Dream Center will always be at the forefront of all of our hearts. The coolest thing is happening – while the team's focus has faithfully stayed on the vision of Pastor Matthew and the local church; God is now blessing and honoring that faithfulness through letting our music reach around the world. With the rotation concept – there are multiple teams that all sound and worship with same like passion and vision of Pastor. Therefore, we are able to help further the awareness of the Dream Center raise funds and meet the demand of God's blessing....without the local church suffering or missing a single beat. I, myself have made a strong commitment to miss very, very few services each year, including vacations and touring. You see, Angelus Temple and the Dream Center is my heart and where your heart is...?

Teaching and scripture reference:

Ephesians 4:1- 6

*2 Be humble and gentle. Be patient with each other, making allowance for each other's faults because of your love. 3 Try always to be led along together by the Holy Spirit and so be at peace with one another. 4 We are all parts of **one body** , we have the same Spirit, and we have all been called to the same glorious future. 5 For us there is only one Lord, one faith, one baptism, 6 and we all have the same God and Father who is over us all and in us all, and living through every part of us.*

TO SUM IT UP ...

NOTES TO SELF...

CHAPTER 4

Worship for 23.5 hours a day... make a joyful noise for 30 minutes!

I believe this is where it's at, right here! Think about it – if our heart is truly in the place it should be. If our heart is honestly in right standings with the Lord. If we have been on our knees. If we have been in the word. If we have been listening to his tender and sovereign voice ....

don't you think that somewhere in there the Lord would have told us to love and care for the people that he gave his life for?

This is something that Pastor Matthew has built the Church and the Dream Center on and we get to reap the benefits of that, with worshippers that GET IT! I believe that the greatest act of worship unto my Lord and Savior, who gave his life for me and the world – is to love and care for people that he loves. Yes, I believe he loves to hear his people calling out to him in praise, worship and honor unto him – but why not just live that all the time? Make it your lifestyle! Constant gratitude, constant praise and constant recognition of his presence!

Then when you and your fellow worshippers come together a few times per week – GO CRAZY in making a joyful noise unto the Lord. The greatest worship can come from the most exhausted and outreach trodden workers and worshippers!

Ask yourself – what would Jesus prefer? For us to sing from our perches called platforms for 23.5 or to serve? It's not how long or how well you worship from the platform that makes you a worshipper, it's how you live your life the other 23.5 hours of the day.

It's not the 30 minutes on stage, it's what you do with the
REST OF YOUR LIFE!

Ask yourself – **WWJD?**

Teaching and Scripture Reference:

Psalms 100 Make a joyful noise...............
Psalms 66
Psalms 95
Psalms 98

TO SUM IT UP ...

NOTES TO SELF...

"Who is the "Worship Team"?

I believe the "Worship Team" is anyone who is involved or has the potential to affect the flow of worship in any given worship service.

IN FACT – not only are they the "Worship Team" – but we consider everyone that has the potential to affect the worship service, is a "Worship LEADER"! Yes, everyone on our team is considered Worship Leaders. I believe in having the entire worship team take the same responsibility of leadership that I do.

Now this will BLOW YOUR MIND! Who is the "Worship Team" and is at every rehearsal, every sound-check? Again, anyone who has the potential of affecting the flow of worship or the service.

Here's who our "Worship Team" or "Worship Leaders" are and I strongly recommend this approach for every church:

- Every Vocalist
- Every Musician
- Every Rotating Worshippers/Leaders/Vocalist/ Musicians
- Every Soundman
- Every Lighting Person
- Every Spot Operator
- Every Computer/ Media/ Power Point, etc/ operators

- Every Camera Person
- Every Video Switcher Operator
- Every Stage Hand
- Every Technical Support Person

Yes, all these people are the "Worship Team" and are expected to be at every rehearsal and every sound-check.

Here is the biggest recommendation! Have a team of total volunteers! If at all possible instill in your worshippers that their participation in the worship services is a gift back to the church and unto the Lord. That keeps their hearts in the right position at all times and truly builds respect for them and your worship, throughout the whole congregation and the staff.

Here is a typical schedule of our weekly rehearsals and service sound-checks; and remember, we rotate all positions.

Wednesday Night:

Rehearsal:
5:30pm - Prayer in the Sanctuary (All worship team members are present)
6:00pm - Vocals go in another room to practice with my wife and I work with the band.
7:00pm - We all come back together in the sanctuary to rehearse the worship material for the entire week's services. The various rotating positions, etc.
(Once a month – we have Motivational Devotions at 7:00pm for 15 minutes)
The rehearsal is usually completed by 9:30pm at the latest.

Thursday Night Service:

3:30pm - Technical crew arrives and does technical
            checks
4:30pm - Musicians and myself go through the entire set
            and transitions
5:15pm - Vocalist arrive and we go through the complete
            set again and final mix.
5:30pm - Technical crew goes through all service cues
            and such as videos, etc.
6:00pm - Stage curtain is closed and Sanctuary is set for
            Pre-service
6:30pm - The entire worship team is in prayer together in
            the green room
6:55pm - Pre-service countdown begins and service
            opening videos are ready
7:00pm - Service starts!

Our other mains services are on:

Saturdays – 7:00pm

Sundays -   10:00am

Note: The report schedules and arrival times are equal to
         Thursday's schedule above.
         3.5 hours prior to any service is when the first
         Technical crew arrive.

TO SUM IT UP ...

If they can affect
the WORSHIP...
they better be on YOUR team!

NOTES TO SELF...

Search for the HEART – not the Talent

One of the most common and frequent questions I get asked is – "How do I select or choose the people on the worship team"?

The answer to that question, without a doubt is – "I look for their HEART first". The Lord has been so faithful in sending us talented people but I have never searched for one. I have only asked that the Lord send us worshippers with a heart for people – not a heart for music and not even a heart for worship – but a heart for people first -and he has truly been so faithful, every time. They must have a heart to serve above anything else.

Oh sure, we get those individuals that come <u>through</u> (underline "THROUGH") that will ask me if they can be on the team. They tell me that they sing or play - that is what the Lord's called them to do – they sing solos – they've done that for every church they've been in. I then always say – "Great, we would love to have you involved! Can you meet us this Sunday morning at 6:30 am to help us get set up for the worship team"? If they say "Absolutely" then there's a great candidate for a worshipper. Unfortunately, more often than not, that is usual the last I hear from them or their passion and desire for worship.

You see, when you have a worshipper who is not consumed with their talents but is more concerned with the hurting and lost people in our community – little petty, pride issues very seldom raise their heads. In fact, when I first interview a potential worshipper and I detect early signs of this issue – I will sometimes tell them, "Your talent is great and I am looking forward to worshipping together, however your talent may be the one thing that stands in the way of us having a lasting relationship. I need your heart to be the predominate thing on your mind and in your motives. In fact if it's OK with you, for the first few services that we rotate you in, there won't be batteries in your mic – is that OK"?

With that approach – we usually get off to a really good start with a clear understanding of what they can expect. Remember, there's strength in numbers and when you've got over 60 people with that same heart and attitude and a Pastor and church reaching out 24/7 – it breeds and creates people with that same passion for people first, worship second and their talents – last! (Remember, worship should be a lifestyle).

How do I select them? One thing that I have found that works, is to actually go out into the congregation after service and recruit them. In other words, I have seen people worshipping the Lord during our worship sets, from their seats. Their act of worship will inspire me to worship and praise my God! I'll then go up to them after church and tell them that they need to be doing that from the platform! They'll usually say something like, "I don't sing" – and I'll say "That's OK, I don't really sing either; but I need people to see you worship the Lord the way I saw you! You made me want to draw closer to him and I couldn't even hear you – but I saw your spirit."….and so on!

I believe in being the most INCLUSIVE team you can. Use your team as an outreach. (read more on this in the chapter – The 4 "E's" of Worship). Select worshippers that have only one motive – people!

Teaching and Scripture Reference:

Matthew 5:8
Blessed are the pure (sincere) in heart…………

TO SUM IT UP ...

NOTES TO SELF...

CHAPTER 7

"Communion" as Worship

It was in a recent service, just after we had ended the worship set and Pastor Matthew was leading and directing the congregation through the traditional Communion segment of that particular Sunday morning. Pastor Matthew was reading from the word and as usual it was pertaining to each of us taking into account our personal relationship with Christ. A time to reflect and ask ourselves if our hearts are right with God, prior to taking the elements of communion. Pastor always uses this time in such a special way in which really causes all Christians and non-Christians to really examine their walk with the Lord.

It is always such a powerful time but this one particular Sunday was different for me personally. This particular call to reflect and examine our walk caused me to totally think of my "Worship" walk in a completely different way. All of a sudden I felt convicted and charged to evaluate and examine my "Worship" walk – before I take of the worship elements every single service. In other words – I made a commitment to really examine my heart, my motives and my heart for God – before I lead anyone or any congregation in the act of corporate worship.

I thought how amazing it would be if I took that same sincerity and devotion of communion and making sure my heart was right before I took of those elements? How much more effective the move of God would be for our congregational worship time, if I took that same passion and reflection upon my heart before taking the physical and spiritual position of directing them to a place in God. A place that I am supposed to have already been. In other words – I can't take them where I haven't already been.

Webster defines "Communion" as - *Intimate fellowship or rapport/ a body of Christians having a common faith and discipline.*

Communication (Communion) is something that everybody does. Our communion and/ or our worship unto the Lord is most important. However, I believe we need to take into account these three areas of communication on an hourly basis.

How do we communicate? Here are three categories or forms of communication that we as worshippers should focus on and take into account on an hourly basis:

"WORDS"
You can learn a lot about people when you listen to them talk. Our words reveal what our minds are thinking. We communicate our thoughts through language. When we speak, we divulge our feelings to others.

You should make a constant assessment of how you are talking. Are your words honest? Are they sincere? Are they polite and respectful of others? Do they edify and encourage?

Have you ever seen someone from a distance before actually meeting them - and think that they are probably really nice and cool people? But then you actually talk to them and within their first ten words from their mouths your opinion of them does a 180? Words are so revealing but that brings me to my next point.

"ACTIONS"
"Actions speak louder than words" Boy do they! We as worshippers must always take into account and make sure our actions are lining up with our words. If we speak positively and encouragingly of others – are our actions

and body language lining up with those words? Or have we just learned what to say instead of being people of integrity? Do our actions show our words to be those of sincerity? On another note - do our actions show those of consistency? In other words – do we stand on the platform, raise our hands, jump around and look and act like shining angelic angels – but then off the platform, our words and actions show a completely different view?

"SPIRIT"

Here's where I believe it all comes down to. I believe the spirit says more than anything. The spirit is that sometimes little thing that communes with others and sometimes it's that huge thing that just screams as it commune with others! The spirit has to be kept in check at all times. I believe that pride is the #1 cause of spirit failures. Don't ever let your spirit get caught up in "Worship Pride", "Church Pride" or just "Christian Pride".

I am an extremely competitive person and I have to continually keep my spirit in check that I don't bring that characteristic into the church and worship settings.   I'll teach more on this in upcoming chapters but here's two things to remember:

- In Man's eyes, there will always be somebody better – In God's eyes, you always be his best!
- Don't compete – one team, one mind and one vision – with all different taste but all in communion with one another.

MAKE SURE ALL 3 THINGS – ALWAYS LINE UP!

Teaching and Scripture References:

1 John 1:7

But if ye walk in the light, as he is in the light, we have fellowship/communion one with another, and the blood of Jesus Christ his son
Cleanseth us from all sin

41

TO SUM IT UP ...

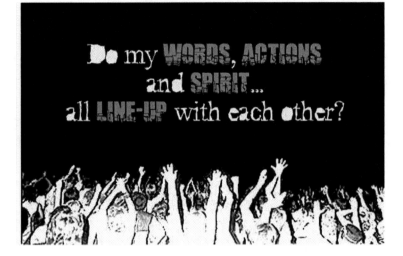

NOTES TO SELF...

Styles of Churches and Worship

I believe this chapter is key to understanding worship and is key to being able to worship the Lord freely. Once your team understands this chapter, I believe it will enable them to not be judgmental of worship styles or worshippers – and that's key!

Have you ever heard these phrases?

- I think worship should be longer.
- I think worship should be spontaneous and flow.
- I think our church should be more worship based.
- I don't think the church should worry so much about the schedule or how polished the service is.

This list could go on and on but this is such an easy thing to answer and clear up. Bottom line – the style, length and direction of your worship service and church service, should line up and reflect the style in which your senior Pastor has received his direction from the Lord.

Don't let yourself get bogged down in comparisons and debates on which is right or wrong. The fact is – there are many different styles of churches that are doing great things for the Lord.

The styles are just that – styles. There are churches built around Faith. Healing, Worship , etc. – Angelus Temple and the Dream Center are built around soul winning and evangelism.

The purpose of our church has been and will remain to be soul winning. However, we have changed the style of our worship and services many times. We have never locked ourselves into a rut or certain style; but have instead always tried to remain current and somewhat ahead, of the latest trends. Without fail, people who return year after year always tell us – "you sound completely different than last year and you really have your own and original sound"! I believe that you should always try to be yourselves and not copy other worship teams. If you like songs from other teams (like PRESS PLAY ☺), then take them and make them even better! If you look at Press Play's last 3 – 4 CD/ DVD projects, you will see four completely different styles, people and each with it's own uniqueness. As many of you have told us – we use to sound black gospel in the beginning, then a little more R&B, then we went through the Psychedelic years, then through the "Only You" club beat years, then the all "White Out" years with an array of everything to where we are now! It's OK to recreate yourself! We always take it as a compliment when people say – "you sound and look nothing like any other team". Be yourself!

What is the style of your church? What is the style and calling of your Pastor? Those two questions are really all that you as a worship leader or worship Pastor have to be concerned with. I believe your responsibility is to your Senior Pastor as unto the Lord.

As long as the hearts behind the Pastor and staff are in line with the word of God, then the different styles that are created from the different personality traits are just that – different styles. There's not one that's more right than another. Don't get me wrong, if you're talking about a wacky cult or something that doesn't line up with the word of God and is preaching something unbiblical – then you know better. But I'm talking about just personality styles, geographical styles or just plain old – "That's the way we do it" - styles.

Don't ever let yourself give too much thought or concern and try to decipher which is right or wrong. If you do, then it's like the days of old when they said "I'm of Paul – I'm of ? Just be the church, the leader and team that God called you to be – but do it under the direction and blessing of your Pastor!

I believe that if you don't agree with the style and direction of your church or it's worship – then you, yes you – is the only thing that needs to change. You need to change your views and quit judging and/or simply move on to another church. It is never your job or anyone else's to change or redirect the direction and calling that the Lord has placed on the Senior Pastor.

As I said in this book earlier, Pastor Matthew has directed this church, Angelus Temple/ The Dream Center to put our focus and efforts on soul winning first. Therefore, everything we do has to lead to one thing and serve one purpose – rescuing the lost.

Our services are designed with the unsaved in mind first! You see, there over 200 ministries that are out in the streets all week long. Turning over boxes, looking under bridges and literally doing everything they can to get the lost souls into the house of God.

Once at church – our job is to close the deal! If I, as a worship leader, was to be on the platform, having my personal spiritual time with Lord – trust me, it would turn off and alienate those lost people from the Lord. Here's why –

You see – I love to worship the Lord. I love to get alone and flow spontaneously! I love to just worship him with no schedule or clock in front of me! In fact, if you ever saw me in my worship closet alone? I like to turn out all the lights, get on the keyboard and just cry and slobber while praising and worshipping my Lord! It's AWESOME!

However – if I did that on the platform in front of people needing a helping hand, an arm around them and a touch from God – don't you think I would send them running out the doors- scared to death of my super-spiritual freak show? See, I don't believe God intended them to be apart of that intimate time, that intimate experience with my creator. That's personal between him and I and should remain so.

If I know the purpose of our church – "Soul Winning" – then my heart should be in the right place and do everything I can to get that hurting person's attention so that they can see God – NOT ME. Right?

It's important that the goal and mission of our church are met so that Pastor is able to bring the word into their open minds and souls. Then when the altar call is given – the deal is closed.

Then the next step for them is the mentoring and discipleship. Now it's time to start the fish cleaning through our various individual programs and ministries that meet throughout the week – targeted to meet their needs and grow them spiritually.

The style of our church services are purposely targeted for the lost first and then our other ministries help develop and train them on their walk with the Lord. You see, when your congregation understands and sees the result of your evangelism throughout the week, unfold before their eyes – they understand and become soul winners along with you. They then realize that the main services are more than just about them and them getting fat from over-feeding – but it's about reaching hurting and lost people.

Teaching and Scripture Reference:

1 Corinthians 1:10-17

10 By the authority of our Lord Jesus Christ I appeal to all of you, my brothers, to agree in what you say, so that there will be no divisions among you. Be completely united, with only one thought and one purpose. 11 For some people from Chloe's family have told me quite plainly, my brothers, that there are quarrels among you. 12 Let me put it this way: each one of you says something different. One says, "I follow Paul"; another, "I follow Apollos"; another, "I follow Peter"; and another, "I follow Christ." 13 Christ has been divided into groups! Was it Paul who died on the cross for you? Were you baptized as Paul's disciples?

15 No one can say, then, that you were baptized as my disciples. 17 Christ did not send me to baptize. He sent me to tell the Good News, and to tell it without using the language of human wisdom, in order to make sure that Christ's death on the cross is not robbed of its power

TO SUM IT UP ...

Let your worship STYLE
not be for and about YOU...
but for and about the LOST.

NOTES TO SELF...

CHAPTER 9

Make Jesus seen and heard... not YOU

Remember the "Invisible Man?" That would be the coolest characteristic that I believe a worshipper could wish for!

I know that our common goal as worshippers is to have Jesus seen and not us. We typically ask for the Lord to use us as open vessels or let us be the conduits that he works through – as the song says "It's all about You, Lord"

So how do we keep ourselves out of the way? Let's be honest – there are a lot of expectations put on a worship team that if not channeled correctly, could be considered as self edifying. I'm sure we've all been tagged with the various titles that people love to hang on worshippers or on the style of the church service. They say things like – "It's very performance driven" or "They're worried about excellence instead of spirit" or "The Lord needs to humble him" or "Their schedule is more important than the moving of God".

These type of opinions will always be where there are people present, so don't ever be discouraged by them and don't let the direction that the Lord and your Pastor has called you to do, be side-tracked. (Read more of this similar topic in the chapter marked "Styles of Churches" – right or wrong).

The challenge is – how do we keep the God given characteristics of being our best, sounding our best, looking our best (which is our expected jobs), how do we not have that come across in our worship. It's easy – first realize that there will always be critics and they usually proclaim to be the most spiritual or they really believe they know what true worship is. SIMPLY IGNORE THEM. They are a non-factor and don't be over obsessed by their opinions or it may become a stronghold in your own life, just pray for them.

Secondly – let the Lord know and your team know, that your heart and goal is to offer the Lord your best. Work hard, rehearse hard and pray harder. That way you are not asking the lord to bless your mess. Then when the work is done (note: Work, I mean hard work, is honorable and accepted in God's eyes. Don't ever let anyone tell you that you should not plan or prepare and you should just let the Lord lead or "Flow". This is probably just my opinion only – so don't write any letters to anyone but me – but I think that's just over-lazy and under-spiritual people trying to prevent something great happening for the Lord; and it's probably due to a pride issue in the lives.)

Sorry – as I'm stepping down off the soap box, I'll continue!

How do you keep God in front of everything else? I believe that you should once again have a team whose heart is for God and the people he died for. You see, I believe that if your church knows that the worship team has been in the streets feeding the hungry all day – they won't be worried about that person's look or sound and be as judgmental. However, if the worship team is not involved in the lives of hurting people – then I believe you are leaving yourself and team as open targets for people's criticism. Remember, people will criticize and their approval cannot be your motivation. You must know what the Lord and your Pastor are expecting of you, for your congregation's style.

Hey for me? I will always rather be criticized for being too professional and an over-prepared steward of what the Lord has called me to do; than the opposite. Remember the chapter - "Worship for 23.5 hours and make a joyful noise for the other half an hour"? That's all you need to worry about! Is your heart right with the Lord and are you living and operating in what (and who) he has called you to serve? If YOU are focused on the Lord – then so will everyone else that sees or hears YOU!

Teaching and Scripture Reference:

Matthew 23: 1-5

23:1 Then Jesus said to the crowds, and to his disciples, 2 "You would think these Jewish leaders and these Pharisees were Moses, the way they keep making up so many laws!
3 And of course you should obey their every whim! It may be all right to do what they say, but above anything else, don't follow their example. For they don't do what they tell you to do.
5 "Everything they do is done for show. They act holy

TO SUM IT UP ...

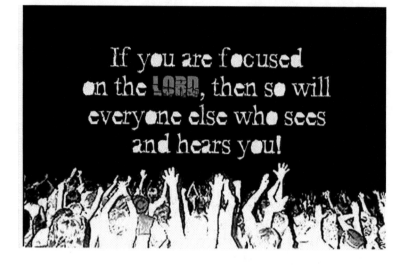

If you are focused
on the LORD, then so will
everyone else who sees
and hears you!

NOTES TO SELF...

CHAPTER 10

What Do You Bring to the Platform?

Here is a letter that I wrote to each of my team members.
If you would like to take this and reformat it for your group,
feel free to do so.

Dear Team,

I am so proud of each of you, the leaders of worship to our
church, community and even our nation. Each of you
continue to lead people into the presence of God by your
own unique expression of love and adoration to our Lord.
I am truly honored to take the platform with you every
week.

I believe as worshippers, the platform is not our right but it
is our divine privilege and honor. Imagine the trust our
Pastor has in you; to allow each of us the privilege of
sharing the platform with him.

With the platform comes a great responsibility and as
leaders in our church, we need to lead the way in showing
Jesus in all that we do. We need to lead the way in our
expression of worship. We need to lead the way in our
sincerity and generosity to the Lord, his church and to one
another. I believe, the responsibility of the platform should
signify to all that "all is well within my soul."

The following things that the Lord laid upon my heart are both spiritual and practical characteristics that I believe are essential for each one of us. I encourage you to go through this check list frequently, as an accountability tool for keeping you in what I am calling "PLATFORM FIT".

That is the challenge I am giving to you...to love the Lord so much, that you are always "PLATFORM FIT".

Here's what we need to bring to the platform:

1. Knowledge of Christ –
   - This sounds basic...and it is! Remember. If it wasn't for Jesus, where would you be? Know and believe that he is the Savior of your soul and that he is the gift – not your talent.
2. Your testimony –
   - What you bring to the platform is fueled by your testimony and it matters! Your testimony will bring passion to your gift.
3. Faith and Expectation –
   - You should be expecting God to do unbelievable things every single service. Your faith should be soaring by the time your feet hit the platform. You are standing in the gap for thousands of people.
4. Joy –
   - The Joy of the Lord must be oozing from your personality and spirit! You must bring JOY to the platform! The people walking through the doors of our church are counting on you to take them away from what they have been going through – and in to the presence of Jesus Christ. It must look like you are happy to be where Jesus is!
5. Passion –
   - Before you even get to the church – let a passion for Christ begin to overwhelm you. Let it be the fuel that drives you. Let that passion be evident!

6. Enthusiasm –
   - Have a burning desire to put your gratefulness and thanksgiving into action. Let what God has done in you be obvious for the person sitting in the very back row to notice. I always say to "Hurt yourself!"

7. Excellence –
   - We serve with excellence because we serve an excellent God! Everybody can do well… but the children of the living God should be able to bring the extraordinary to the platform.

8. Service –
   - Be dedicated to serve. Being dedicated to HIS service brings a joy that you do not find outside HIS purpose. Love to serve the Lord, Pastor Matthew, our church and each other.

9. Unity –
   - Unity is not just something you bring to the platform…it is essential! Make every effort… that means you have to do something, to keep unity always prevalent. Unity does not come by chance, it does not come without work and it does not come without dying to self daily.

10. Generosity –
    - As Darlene Zschech said – be generous in your worship. You can't out worship or over worship God. Go crazy and express your love with all that is within you! Give him everything and you will be blessed.

11. Ears and Eyes –
    - This means you have to keep your head in the game! Be prepared! Give God your best, don't ever wing it and think that it's spiritual. By all means – have your spiritual head in the game – above all, be spiritually prepared!!!

#12 – You must have your…….

TOUR GUIDE CREDENTIALS!!!

Take them on a Journey to Christ!

- You can only take someone to where you have already been. So get everything in your heart, mind and soul pure before the Lord and take them into the Holy of Holies. Live in his presence, dwell in his presence 24 hours a day!

Teaching and Scripture Reference:

Philippians 4:8

Finally, brethren, whatever things are true, whatever things are noble, whatever things are just, whatever things are pure, whatever things are lovely, whatever things are of good report, if there is any virtue and if there is anything praiseworthy — meditate on these things. 9 The things which you learned and received and heard and saw in me, these do, and the God of peace will be with you.

TO SUM IT UP ...

NOTES TO SELF...

_____

_____

_____

_____

_____

_____

_____

_____

_____

_____

_____

_____

_____

_____

_____

_____

_____

_____

"PRAYER" – you can't get closer to God without it.

Prayer is definitely the key to everything. Prayer is that one thing that there is no substitute for. Prayer is one of those things that you can definitely not do too much of.....or can you?

I thought that might be a good attention getter to start this chapter. Honestly, prayer is the most important thing that you can do for it is the act of communion with your creator. There should be no substitute for it and prayer can never be ignored or replaced.

You know I hear the terms "Going to the next Level" and "Getting closer to God" said continually. I don't believe that it is at all possible to accomplish either phrase without prayer. This chapter is definitely for me, one of the most convicting chapters; because honestly, I never have felt like I have been where I'm supposed to be in my prayer life. I know that sounds bad but honestly, no matter where I have been in my relationship with the Lord, have I ever really felt that I have done all I can with my prayer time and discipline.

I don't know if you have ever felt that way too; but it almost became another one of those unsurpassable hurdles in my walk. I begin to wonder, that if someone could never pray enough and spend time on their knees with the Lord – then my walk with him must really be bad. I could never measure up to this prayer burden that I was putting on myself.

Then I begin to realize another freedom key! Just as worship – I should spend every hour of every day in constant communion with him, not just a few minutes on my knees physically. All I have to do is make a continued acknowledgement of his presence and live my life in the understanding that he is with me at all times – therefore, talk to him – yes, all the time. I don't mean weird and out loud where people not only wonder if you're off your rocker but you confirm it. No, I mean through that still small voice that he speaks to you in – just speak and acknowledge him right back. Make him a part of everything!

Can you pray too much? I hope you take this in the right way – I believe you can pray too much if all you do is pray and there is no action to that prayer. In other words – usually for me, prayer motivates me to get off my knees and go help someone in need; or to show someone overwhelming, unconditional love. Therefore, I've never understood those who pray for hours upon hours but they never seem to physically go and help those who Christ died for. If their prayer time becomes their replacement for what God has called each of us to do; and that is to love and care for the hurting – then yes. In my opinion, that person is praying too much and they should just get up and do it.

Moving on! As a worshipper, prayer should be the steady in your life. It should be the one thing that you don't compromise in. I encourage you to live this and teach this to everyone within your group and team.

Make it simple and non-intimidating! Prayer does not have to be hard or super spiritual. I don't believe there are rookies in this area. It's kind of like "True Worship." Prayer, the words and how of what you express to your creator for the very first time – could be more real and special to God than any experience prayer warrior's. I don't believe that to God, one is better or more special than the other. He knows the heart and the motive and sincerity behind it.

Just teach your team to begin praying! If they're not "experienced" pray-ers – just have them start by being grateful and thankful for everything. Teach them to pray through an act of thanksgiving unto their Savior. Show them, start a simple prayer and just show them how to start a prayer of gratitude unto the Lord. "Thank you Jesus for saving my life", "Thank you Jesus for giving me another day." The list will be endless and pretty soon they will catch on that the Lord is just wanting communion with them and then they will desire to know more about him.

"Prayer Stoppers"
Teach them about Prayer Stoppers. I don't know about you but there are things that causes me to stop praying. There are things and circumstances that causes me to pull back from being disciplined in my prayer life. I call them Prayer Stoppers. No, I don't mean your mother-in-law or that lovely old deacon! I mean things in your heart and walk that allow you to feel distant from God.

Here's a few "Prayer Stoppers":

- Disobedience to the Lord
- Rebellion
- Lack of Faith
- Bitterness/ Un-forgiveness
- Besetting Sins

I believe that we can be our own biggest prayer stoppers. We disconnect ourselves from the one thing that connects us to God. You see, God doesn't change but when we take a step away from him – we tend to have a tougher time bringing ourselves back into communion with him. I believe that guilt plays a big role in stopping us from pressing back in again.

Be closer to God today, than you were yesterday!

Be in constant communion with Him!

Teaching and Scripture Reference:

James 4:8
8 And when you draw close to God, God will draw close to you.

Matthew 6:15
9 " Pray, then, in this way:
'Our Father who is in heaven,
Hallowed be Your name.
10' Your kingdom come.
Your will be done,
On earth as it is in heaven.
11' Give us this day our daily bread.
12' And forgive us our debts, as we also
have forgiven our debtors.
13' And do not lead us into temptation, but
deliver us from evil. [For Yours is the
kingdom and the power and the glory
forever. Amen.']
14 " For if you forgive others for their
transgressions, your heavenly Father will
also forgive you. 15 "But if you do not
forgive others, then your Father will not
forgive your transgressions.

TO SUM IT UP ...

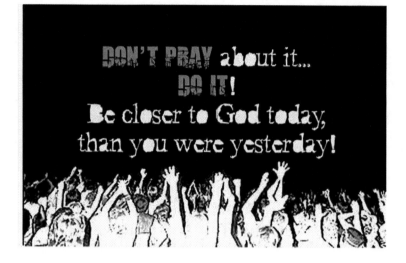

NOTES TO SELF...

Run a tight ship – but don't OWN the ship!

I have been blessed and honored to be able to serve under such an incredible leader as Pastor Matthew Barnett. He is truly an amazing leader and if I have learned anything, that is to run a tight ship – but don't own the ship!

Pastor Matthew and his father are the most "Permission" giving leaders and Pastors that I have ever met. There are so many blessing that I have in life and working under a leadership style as theirs, is one of the greatest.

You don't have to spend much time at Angelus Temple or on the campus of the Dream Center to recognize that everything is attempted to be done in a spirit of excellence. From every department and every ministry leader, there is a goal and conviction of doing everything for the Lord with a spirit and stewardship of excellence.

I take that same approach and spirit with the worship and music team of the two campuses. I teach and promote extreme commitments from everybody involved within the areas of my oversight. I believe in wearing many hats and I am so glad that I have the privilege of overseeing the numerous departments that I do. If your church does not have the Worship Director oversee the various departments that I do – there's nothing wrong with that.

Every church is different but I am just glad that several of the departments that have to do with the flow and organization of the services, are at my responsibility to oversee but more importantly - to serve.

As these two great organizations grow(Angelus Temple / The Dream Center) roles and duties are ever changing. The Lord has truly blessed by raising up and continuing to send other great Pastors and leaders to help divide up the responsibilities of both campuses. In the last year it seems that I have been blessed in being able to focus on Worship, music and the connected departments more than I ever have before. As a result, I believe that the Lord is allowing a fresh move of worship throughout our congregation like never before.

I am a very, very hands on type of leader. I believe that if my responsibility is the flow and organization of the services, then I need and am honored to train and oversee anything that could affect or influence that flow. Therefore, I oversee on a daily basis the following departments:

- Worship Leading (Directing, leading, writing, training, planning, etc.)
- Music Department (Music office, teaching, resources, etc.)
- Media Department (Cameras, staffing, duplication, etc.)
- Editing Department (Video Announcements, Worship visuals, Illustrated Sermon video, random videos)
- Audio Department (Sound, staffing, maintenance, scheduling, etc.)
- Lighting Department (Lighting, staffing, maintenance, scheduling, etc.)
- IMAG/ Video (Everything that goes to screens, videos, backgrounds, scriptures, etc.)
- Television Shows – currently on TBN, Daystar, Cornerstone(Producer that oversees the content, editing, shooting and scheduling)
- Staging and Design
- Props and warehousing

The way I oversee all this is very hands on but at the same time – very hands off. I want to encourage and promote creativity and freedom within the workers so that they feel a part of the plan, vision and the big picture. I'll organize it tightly but allow them the freedom to bring it to pass. I usually already know how I want something to look or sound like before I give it to them to do – and there's the tricky part. I have to be careful right then and there to let them first take a chance at the creativity end before I tell them the way to do it. Does that make sense? In other words – if I know they need or are expecting detailed directions and input from me, then I give it to them just that way – and they tease me that they had better be writing it down quickly as my minds spits it all out in an array of color, sound and detail. However, if it's something that I know their own passion is in and that it's not just a job they have to do – then I'll throw out the basic concept of what I need and by when and tell them to surprise me. Then, I'll look at the first few hours of work to make sure they're on the right track before I waste their or the churches time. Then I monitor the progress closely.

Again I say! USE YOUNG PEOPLE! They are the easiest to train, schedule and they always seem to have great attitudes. They're never set in their ways and they are very flexible. Let's face it – they already know a lot more than most of us!

Young people are so easy to have fun with and I believe in that! I didn't always have fun – some would think I still don't! But have fun doing this type of ministry. These departments should represent the fun, excitement, passion and energy of the whole church. Be organized but have FUN! Be Inclusive – get everybody you can involved!

Read more on this concept in the chapter on the 4 "E's" of Worship (Excellence).

Teaching and Scripture Reference:

Ephesians 2:10

"*For we are God's workmanship, created in Christ Jesus to do good works, which God prepared in advance for us to do.*"

TO SUM IT UP ...

NOTES TO SELF...

CHAPTER 13

Be friends with everyone.....
but ASSOCIATE with the strong!

The worshipper's life should be above approach! That's a tall order to live up to! However, I believe it can only be accomplished when healthy associations are present.

As worshippers, we always say we want to draw closer to God and go to the next level – I believe it will depend greatly on your associations, your friends or the people you hang with the most.

What is a HEALTHY relationship or association? An association that you can without a doubt know and say, that both parties are better people as a result of that relationship.

Here are four areas, that if your worship team and youth group can grasp and put into practice – it will revolutionize the unity and freedom in your church.

1. Commit to be involved with relationships that are spiritually sound. For me personally, to get close to God, sometimes I have to withdraw myself from certain people. I know that Christ loves all and wants us to also – but I know that I also have to pull back from certain personality and character types; in order for me to get a clear perspective of Christ.

When you get close to someone, you can't help but mimic them. When you get close to God, you mimic him. Sometimes there's just certain people that would rather you not mimic God.

2. Commit to NOT being involved with relationships that are self-serving. In a self-serving relationship, you are generally in it for what you can get out of the relationship. In a lot of instances, these are the associations that aren't generally our first choice in the selection process but you compromise your standards for what that experience may bring you.

3. Watch out for relationships that start healthy but are slowly weakening your spiritual walk. Watch out for these types because they are stealth like in their influences and here are a few signs to watch for and avoid being close to people with these characteristics:

  - Ones that you leave the experience just not feeling right about.
  - People that are negative about other people, ministry, fellow Christians or Pastors.
  - Compromisers.
  - Extreme Intellectuals.
  - Discouraged or very needy.
  - Controlling.

Now of course, we are to love and minister to all people including the above type. However, as worshippers you need to always guard your heart from other's characteristics that will just bring you down.

You see, our walk with Christ and our acts of worship are done so through faith and our belief and trust in Jesus Christ. The above characteristic types depend only on their feeling, their thoughts, their minds or their pride.

4. We must always ask ourselves – Where is Christ in our Relationships? Now this is where I am as guilty as anyone. Am I really taking Christ with me in to every single association I have? I believe that if I just take the first step to walk away from the wrong ones and walk in to the right ones, then the Lord is always faithful and will bless your pro-activeness. I don't believe you can ride the fence and be two different people and have a close relationship with Christ. Be balanced though….in the right way.

BE A POSITIVE INFLUENCE EVERY TIME!!!

I encourage you to also contact our Youth Pastors – **Brad and Stella Reed**. Brad spoke so effectively in a recent service on this very subject and would be able to give you added material and teachings!

Teaching References:

Romans 16:17-18

17 I urge you, brothers, to watch out for those who cause divisions and put obstacles in your way that are contrary to the teaching you have learned. Keep away from them. 18 For such people are not serving our Lord Christ, but their own appetites. By smooth talk and flattery they deceive the minds of naive people.

TO SUM IT UP ...

I just want to reach out and be a light in their darkness... YEAH RIGHT!

NOTES TO SELF...

CHAPTER 14

Characteristics of a healthy worshipper
and
Characteristics of a great leader.

- Praises other people frequently, even when praise is not deserved.
- Is the example and refers to those above or below him, as greater examples.
- Is and shows genuine excitement and joy for other's successes.
- An effective leader builds and recognizes other staff and fellow worshippers over himself.
- An effective leader will never engage in clicks or gossip with or about other leaders and fellow worshippers.
- Will out work his teammates and be the first one there and the last one to leave.

ABOVE ALL – a true, honest, selfless, sincere and effective leader – UNIFIES!

Now do this – change the word "Leader" to "Follower" and see that they equally carry the same characteristics. I believe, in order to be an effective worshipper or an effective leader – you must equally focus on being a follower. I don't know of anyone more pliable and ready to learn from others, than Pastor Matthew. He'll be the first to examine others and new ways of doing things. He is the greatest example of being a leader and he is the greatest example of being a follower.

Look at the similarities:

- An effective follower, praises other people frequently, even when not deserved.
- An effective follower is the example and refers to those or below him, as greater examples.
- An effective follower, is and shows genuine excitement and joy for other's successes.
- An effective follower, builds and recognizes other staff and fellow worshippers over himself.
- An effective follower, will never engage in clicks or gossip with or about other leaders and fellow worshippers.
- An effective follower, will out work his teammates and be the first one there and the last to leave.

Teaching and Scripture Reference:

2 Peter 1:5

For this very reason, make every effort to add to your faith goodness; and to goodness knowledge, self-control; and to self-control, perseverance; and to perseverance, godliness;
7 and to godliness, brotherly kindness; and to brotherly kindness, love.
8 For if you possess these qualities in increasing measure, they will keep you from being ineffective and unproductive in your knowledge of out Lord Jesus Christ. 9 But if anyone does not have them, he is nearsighted and blind, an has forgotten that he has been cleansed form his past sins.

TO SUM IT UP ...

A true, honest, selfless, sincere and effective leader...
...UNIFIES!

NOTES TO SELF...

No more DRAMA!

In the words of a great lyrist – "No More DRAMA"!
Although that song was not a Christian or Worship song –
the person who wrote it must had been on a worship team!

Thank the Lord that we are blessed with the greatest of
worshippers with the right HEARTS! However, there are
times that the Drama Queens seem to be gathering for
their conventions or that their theme song changes to
Janet Jackson's - "What Have You Done For Me Lately?"

Obviously, we're talking and dealing with the issue of pride
and jealousy. Unfortunately, these two things raise their
heads in each of us if we let them. Whether, we want to
admit it, we all deal with pride and jealousy on some level.
The amount that it consumes our thoughts, minds, motives
and spirits is the real question.

Again, I come back to the solution instead of the problem.
There's no need in identifying the people with these issues
– because they're obvious. In an environment of servant-
ship, they stick out like soar thumbs!

Therefore, if you don't want drama in your youth group or
on your worship team – have a team of servants! Show
your team how to serve! Go with them and out serve
them.

We don't need to spend much time on this topic because I believe that you need to practice ignoring the drama queens and focus on the positive – JESUS!

The only DRAMA that should be on your team – is the drama of who is going to out serve!

Teaching and Scripture Reference:

Philippians 3:12-15

*12 I don't mean to say that I have already achieved these things or that I have already reached perfection! But I keep working toward that day when I will finally be all that Christ Jesus saved me for and wants me to be. 13 No, dear brothers and sisters, **I am still not all I should be, but I am focusing all my energies on this one thing: Forgetting the past and looking forward to what lies ahead,** 14 I strain to reach the end of the race and receive the prize for which God, through Christ Jesus, is calling us up to heaven.*
*15 **I hope all of you who are mature Christians will agree on these things. If you disagree on some point, I believe God will make it plain to you.***

TO SUM IT UP ...

NOTES TO SELF...

Views on "Secular Music"

I was contemplating on whether I even wanted to touch this subject – but I hope my views will help you. I won't spend much time on this topic because honestly – it's not a topic, or at least it's not made into a big deal – here's what I mean –

There was a period of my life, a few years ago, that I refrained from listening to any and all secular music. It was a period of my life that previously my walk with the Lord had slipped backwards and I personally had drifted from the disciplined life of operating in the Lord's fullness. Therefore, I felt it necessary for a period of time to withdraw myself from all music that didn't have a Christian message.

You see, I feel that in all things, there may be things or situations that the Lord will urge you to go on somewhat of a fast – of anything! If we're honest with ourselves, we know when we are allowing things to influence our walk with God. We know when we somewhat begin to worship things other than what's healthy. It happens to all of us I believe, in one way or another, whether it's sports, friends or entertainment – we can get just too carried away with things.

Here's what I teach our team – Make sure your own personal walk with the Lord is strong enough that

NOTHING will influence you or distract you from the glory of God. You see, the words or lyrics to someone else's song; wasn't the reason that I compromised my walk with the Lord. I compromised my walk with the Lord because I chose to not live daily in his presence and in constant communion with him. I want our team to be spiritually sound and strong enough that we can walk into any secular restaurant or shopping mall and our walk with the Lord will not feel threatened at all. You see, I believe my God is stronger than all that and I just stay close to the strong one.

Now of course if the lyrics of a song are explicit or just not right then I just flat turn it off – in fact, it usually just makes me mad and irritated that those unintelligent writers couldn't come up with something more creative than uneducated trailer trash. See, I have a strong opinion!

As I said in the chapter of "True Worship" – we are a soul winning church and will have 100 – 1000 unsaved people in every service, every week. In fact, we do not feel we are doing our jobs of outreach unless the lost are in great numbers every service. Therefore, if using a guitar intro from a secular tune will help me get the attention of the unsaved – then yes, I'll do it! Honestly though – it's usually the holy and sanctified Christians that recognize and enjoy those intros more than anyone! ☺ Hey, the method is not sacred – the message is!

Teaching and Scripture Reference:

Psalms 40:3

He has PUT a NEW SONG in my mouth, even Praise
unto our God: that many may see it, and trust in
the Lord

TO SUM IT UP ...

NOTES TO SELF...

CHAPTER 17

Five Basic Principles

1. Always know and follow the direction of your Senior Pastor.

2. Faithfully serve your immediate leaders and pray for them daily.

3. Show the way – you can't ask someone to follow where you haven't been.

4. Unify, in all that you do – let everything you do always direct people to Jesus and to the direction of the church in which the Lord has placed you.

5. There's no way to live for Jesus, without living for others.

NOTES TO SELF...

Do songs from <u>YOUR</u> church!

One of the most inspiring and exciting things that can occur in your worship and in your church – is to birth songs from the heart of the worshippers in <u>your</u> team and church!

As I said in previous chapters, I believe that there is something very special to having the privilege of songs being birthed from your own individual team members. There's something special that not only brings ownership for your team but your congregation seem to adopt those songs as their own as well.

The ownership I'm talking about is not about "Owning" the song – It's about owning it in the sense that it came straight from the Lord to the heart of you, your team member and to your congregation. It's you, your team and the congregation knowing and seeing the evidence that time was spent with the Lord.

Of course, you have to do a lot of material and I totally recommend that you do the songs and material that best fits your church, regardless of the writer but encourage your team to write.

I encourage everybody on our team that feels they are called and gifted to write, to submit their material to me. I tell them that there are a few guidelines to think about before submitting them:

- First make sure the song is in the style of worship that we already do. The song must fit our style and the church's style.

- Make sure that it's something you can see and hear me (the worship leader) doing.

- I would love to do every song that is brought to me – but the fact is I can't. Therefore, prepare yourself not to be disappointed if we don't do it. It doesn't mean that it's not a great song.

- I always tell them that I myself, don't do every song that I personally write either. It usually takes throwing a lot of songs at the wall, for one good one to stick.

Now I also have recommendations and guidelines for the team and/ or band and vocals; upon listening to the proposed material. In other words, when a team member is auditioning their new, original song to us and the other team members – I have a few recommendations to the listeners, the team who is getting to review or hear this auditioning song:

- First, no matter how good or how bad the song sounds the first time you hear it – always compliment and brag on it. Smile and nod your head like you love it no matter what.

- Be careful not to send off any negative body language like frowns, rolling of the eyes, etc.

- Give the song a second and third chance before pre-judging it.

- Don't say to the writer or anyone else – "Oh this song sounds like this other song". Remember, God was the only original being. Every song is going to sound like another song in some way, however I don't believe in stealing and copying material either. Just give the writer the benefit of the doubt and let the song take form before casting it down.

- You, yes you – make the song sound good. Whether you like it or not, you the players and singers, make it sound great. Try you hardest, do your best. I've seen some great songs never make it out of the gate because the band wasn't enthused at it's conception.

- I say this again – Compliment – Compliment. Remember, you like to be complimented on your guitar solos or vocal solos, don't you? If you were bringing a new song – you would want to be complimented, right? So throw the writer a bone! Lavish them with praise, encourage them – it may be <u>you</u> needing that bone the next service!

Remember, as a writer – this is the most terrifying and intimidating thing to go through. If you as the listener are not prayed up and are in control of yourself – you could possibly be responsible for discouraging a person from doing what the Lord called them to do.

ABOVE ALL!
1. Ask the Lord to anoint you and your songs!
2. Relax and enjoy the entire writing, auditioning and listening process!

Teaching and Scripture Reference:

Psalms 96:1- 4
Sing a new song to the LORD!
Let the whole earth sing to the LORD!
2 Sing to the LORD; bless his name.
Each day proclaim the good news that he saves.
3 Publish his glorious deeds among the nations.

Tell everyone about the amazing things he does.
4 Great is the LORD! He is most worthy of praise!

TO SUM IT UP ...

NOTES TO SELF...

Show me a sincere worshipper… and I'll show you a… HUMBLE SERVANT

Thankful, Grateful, Generous, Encourager and Kind – those are all words that describe a sincere worshipper. Those are all words that describe a humble servant.

I believe the greatest attribute of a sincere worshipper is that of a sincere humble spirit. If there was anything that I feel is necessary but also very hard to keep accountable in – that is having sincere humility.

I guess it's just human nature and actually the result of good intentions; but false humility just bugs me. Have I been guilty of it? Absolutely! However, I have found that if I stay close to God, read his word faithfully and serve the people he loves – then he keeps me accountable when a phony or false humility tries to raise it's head.

I think sometimes as worshippers – because people are so nice and sometimes they can shower us with praise and compliments, we in turn sometimes can act over humble instead of just thanking them and giving God the glory for it. You know what I mean?

Then on another completely different side of it – there are those worshippers, who walk close to God, read the word faithfully and even serve hurting people – but yet they think they are perfect. Have you ever met those? It makes you wonder which scriptures they're reading?

I mean they are great people! Smart, sometimes too smart; but just good people. Did well in school, loves God and love people – but they are the first ones to tell you just how great they are!

If you have those type of people on your team – just pray for them and encourage them to realize that everything they are and do is because of Christ and not them. That it is Jesus working through them and not themselves. Teach them and show them how important it is for worshippers to have sincere humility.

Teaching and Scripture Reference:

Matthew 20: 26 & 27

.......whoever wants to become great among you must be your servant, 27 and whoever wants to be first must be your slave – 28 just as the Son of Man did not come to be served, but to serve, and to give his life as a ransom for many."

TO SUM IT UP ...

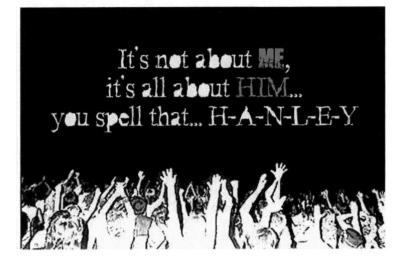

It's not about ME,
it's all about HIM...
you spell that... H-A-N-L-E-Y

NOTES TO SELF...

HOW TO MAKE -
"Service Opening Videos"

I am such a believer in first impressions. I believe that from the parking lot to the greeters – the impression people receive when arriving to the church should reflect our faithful stewardship to our calling.

In the same respect – I believe the very first impression of the service should be sharp, exciting and reflect faithfulness.

Opening Videos, I feel are a must! They can be anything you want them to be. We make our opening videos ourselves and make them in a way that is like a quick promo of our church or is an introduction to that particular service, topic or event.

1) First I choose the music under the opening video. This music should be the same music of your first opening live song, in your worship set and/or start with different music and then transition into the first song; before the live band starts. I usually only do the intro and first verse as the opening video and then come LIVE at the top of the chorus. If you have your own CDs of your worship team or DVDs, then use that music. If you don't have that – then use the songs from other CDs and DVDs, such as United/ Hillsong or PRESS PLAY! ☺

2) Then put your music audio into your video editing software. Now begin to add video shots, pictures of what ever you see or want the audience to see. Be

imaginative and creative. Go back and forth from your local church video footage and that of the worship DVD, to show crowds and excitement.

3) In addition to music and video – I like to use a voice-over to draw their attention. Just find people in your church who have an exciting and clear voice to do this.

4) Your video is now ready for use – go to a black-out with all lights – roll the video – band is getting in place while the video rolls – vocals are getting in place – then as the chorus hits – the lights and auditorium explodes in awesome praise!

TO SUM IT UP ...

You only have one chance,
to make a first impression.
Is it worth a SOUL to YOU?

NOTES TO SELF...

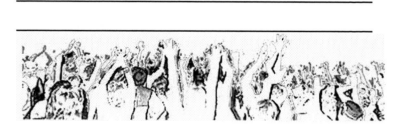

HOW TO MAKE –
"Transition Videos"

Transitions Videos are the greatest tool to use in between your fast songs, going into your slow songs. In other words – if you need something to break up the craziness from your fast, praise, jumping songs into your slow worship – here's your answer.

1) Whatever the message, topic or title of your first slow worship song is – make a testimonial video to play before that song.

2) With any video camera – go shoot about 8 different 15 second testimonials from people within your youth group and church. (For main services, it's good to use all age groups to better relate to all).

3) The content of their testimonies should be about that next songs topic, applied to their lives. Here's an example: Let's say your first slow song is "Here I Am to Worship" and the first line says "Light of the World…"etc. You would then direct them to use terms such as "I thank the Lord for always being there for me and for coming to help lift me out of darkness, etc" The next one would say – "Jesus

has truly been the light in my world" etc… and so on..

4) Then edit all of them down and take just the best. I recommend that the total length of the video is only 60 – 90 seconds. I like to use the black and white effect for these videos.

5) You don't need music on the video – instead the keys or a guitar plays that actual song LIVE under the video. That way you're already in the actual key and song, so that – as soon as the Transition Video is done – you vocally and musically flow right into that same message and song with worship. This is where we sometimes roll out the grand piano or B3, during these videos, while their attention is on the video testimonials. Remember, the Transition Video should start right at the end of your last fast song.

6) The greatest thing about these videos is that it is exciting and inclusive for your whole congregation because you're using them, the congregation to be a part of speaking into people's lives. I use not only the congregation but also people within the worship team too. It's good for everyone to hear the wonderful works of the Lord!

TO SUM IT UP ...

NOTES TO SELF...

Early is ON TIME…on time is LATE!

This is a great thing to teach your youth group, your staff and especially your worship team! It is so easy to teach them and really brings a clear understanding of giving God our best.

Since I'm a musician/ singer or "Artist" – then I can pick on them! I don't believe in the stereo-type character flaw that all musicians or artist, just run late to everything. Oh I've seen plenty that do and I just don't accept that as being or having a Christ-like character. If anything, I believe and expect our worship team members to be the example in running on time, both in our services, rehearsal etc. – but especially in their personal lives. I am not one of those that accepts that it's just "the way they are." To me, it's a character flaw just like any other short-coming that people allow to creep into their lives.

Here's why – if I commit with my words to be somewhere at a particular time; and I am not there – then what happened? Oh I understand traffic, car accident and the other 3 million excuses that I know we've all heard – but if it seems to be a pattern in their life – then there's a significant problem and it won't be tolerated. In other words – when we accept a person to be on the team, there is a schedule commitment that they commit to. With their words they say YES – I can do it – I'll be there! When they're not – they have a character problem!

Yes, I'm pretty cut and dry, black and white on this issue! I guess you can tell? Here's why I just don't buy it – I don't know of anyone busier than Pastor Matthew Barnett – but guess what? He is NEVER late to anything! How can that be? Is the traffic just pulling over to the side of the road for him? No – he's decided to be a man of his word! I'm busier than a one-arm, paper hanger, in a wind storm – but I am early to everything! How can that be? Is my "Jetson" helicopter just faster than everyone else's? No – I respect my commitments. Whether those commitments are to be at worship practice, sound-check, church or to my wife's dinner engagement – I believe in respecting the things that the Lord has blessed me with, enough to keep my commitments.

Therefore, our worship team and pretty much our entire church – lives by "Early is ON TIME...on time is LATE! Meaning this – if sound-check is at 4:30pm, then if they show up at 4:30 – then they're late – because sound-check is at 4:30, not showing up. Therefore, they would need to show up as early as it takes them to be plugged-in, tuned up and prepared for playing the sound-check at 4:30! They love me! But that's how we operate and give God our best. A minimum of five minutes early is expected and that's ON TIME.

No matter who or what they do, be it vocals, musicians or technical crews – Early is ON TIME... on time LATE! No exceptions.

I CORINTHIANS 10:31

Whatever you do, do it all for the Glory of God

ECCLESIASTES 9:10

Whatsoever thy hand findeth to do, do it with thy might

TO SUM IT UP ...

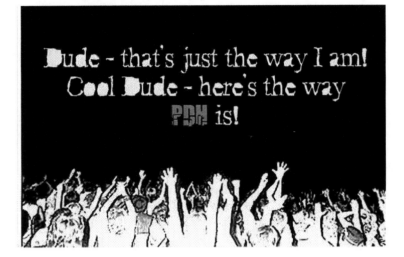

NOTES TO SELF...

SERVING is the greatest form of Worship!

If you have noticed, there is one common thread and message that is woven throughout this book. In fact, it's that one common message that Angelus Temple and the Dream Center is built upon; and that is SERVANT-SHIP.

Without a doubt, I believe serving IS the greatest form of worship! Whether you are serving hurting and lost people or serving the Pastor and staff that the Lord has called you to – you must have the heart of servant-ship to be effective as a worshipper.

You see, I feel that the heart of a worshipper is a heart of thanksgiving, gratitude, stewardship and generosity. In all those attributes, there must be a serving mind set and heart for them to exist. When you are thankful for what the Lord has done for you and for what he's given you – you want to serve other people. When you are grateful for all his blessings and provision – you want to serve other people. When you are faithful with what the Lord's given to you – you want to serve and bless others with it. When you realize all that he has given you and in the abundance that he has given life to you – you can't help but be a generous person to others.

As you can see, WORSHIP is Christ like and is the farthest thing from selfishness. They are at completely opposite

115

ends of the spectrum. I don't believe you can be self thinking, ungrateful and withholding; and call yourself a true God loving and God pleasing worshipper. If your heart is for God and you truly know him in an intimate way – then you will be the first to know that his interest and passion is for people- the people he created and gave his life for.

Serve with all your heart! Never stop sacrificing for others. Never stop giving to others. Never stop doing your very best as an offering unto the Lord. In everything you do – do it with all your heart. Keep you HEART in a servant-ship mentality. Build up others, compliment others and help promote others to their divine purpose. In all that you're doing, ask yourself if you are serving others – before you are serving yourself.

Serving is what I was talking about when I wrote "Worship for 23.5 Hours a Day….make a Joyful Noise for 30 minutes. Meaning that it doesn't matter the length of your worship service, the level of sound, the height you jump or don't jump, the amount of space you give for spontaneous flowing, or really the level that you think you are a Christian and are worshipping God. If your heart is right – then you will be serving people! Period!

If you really love the Lord and really love Worship – then you will love to worship him through serving him and also giving of yourself and time – to the people that he gave himself for.

Teaching References:

Matthew 20:28

"just as the Son of Man did not come to be served, but to serve , and to give his life as a ransom for many."

I Peter 4:10

Each one should use whatever gift he has received to serve others, faithfully administering God's grace in its various forms.

John 15:12-13

My command is this: Love each other as I have loved you. 13 Greater love has no one than this, that he lay down his life for his friends.

TO SUM IT UP ...

Ask yourself...
am I always serving others,
BEFORE myself?

NOTES TO SELF...

Never say NO!

Be your Pastor's "GO TO" team! Your entire team of worshippers should be your Pastor's "GO TO" team for anything and at any time, that he should need. Even if it's not related to music, teach your team to serve your Pastor in every capacity possible – and if it is related to music - be your Pastor's own personal "Karaoke" machine! Yes – be his Karaoke machine!

If your Pastor asks for a particular song, style or arrangement – do it! Don't ever say NO! I'm serious, I have never told Pastor Matthew "NO" on anything that I can remember; and trust me, with Pastor Matthew's vision and imagination – there have been some incredible requests!

Here's how I serve him in this capacity – let's say he may ask for a particular song at the last minute. I'll always say to him, "Absolutely, we can do it" and then if I don't feel that it will be it's best because of lack of rehearsal, or something that he would be embarrassed by, then I will warn or tell him that and let him make the call. Then if he says to go ahead and do it – then I will make sure to impress his socks off by how great it was, without any rehearsal! I will never do it and make him regret his decision. The greatest thing you can do is to make every decision of his, look like the best decision ever! Get there earlier than normal to rehearse it, do what ever you have to and make it come off incredibly spectacular!

Now when it comes to your Pastor requesting various songs from various artist and styles – again always say YES! This is another example of when you can personally put into practice, what you preach. Don't let the style of the music requested mean too much to you. In other words, if the song or styles of material that he is requesting, is something you really personally don't like – do it anyway and make it spectacular. Remember, if your heart is to serve him and the congregation that you have been called to – then trust me, there will be several people who <u>does</u> like that song or style. Don't let your personal opinions (or PRIDE) get in the way of what the Lord wants to do through your Pastor and through you.

I've also been asked what to do in this situation. Let's say that your Pastor may ask you to use certain individuals in the church or even outside the church, that you feel shouldn't be used because of whatever you may know about them, etc. Well this is an easy answer – relax! It's not your duty to worry or judge his calls! I personally can't remember a particular situation that I didn't agree with Pastor on in this area. In fact, he is usually very permission-giving but at the same time very sensitive to who I use on the platform. However, if this situation did occur? The answer is still easy – I'd do whatever he asked and I would make that person look and sound great!

You see, I put my trust totally in God and God is the one that Pastor answers to, not ME! Therefore, I can relax and just serve my Pastor's socks off and he knows that I'm never judging or questioning his vision or decision making.

It is such an incredible blessing to be serving under a Pastor like Matthew Barnett; because it's evident that he is listening and trusting God every single day. How can I never say NO? Because I trust Pastor Matthew 100%. For me there is no question of where my place is - and what my duties are - and where my service and loyalty is…..it's with God and the people he has placed me under.

If you find yourself in a constant struggle with this type of servant-ship. If you are struggling with totally surrendering your will and you can't find it easy to trust and serve your Pastor with the "Never say NO" approach – then I encourage you to <u>change</u>.

Yes you! No matter what the situation, you and I can always move closer to God and move farther away from our own personal motives or opinions. Ask God to allow you to see things from his and your Pastor's point of view. Allow yourself room to grow and to evolve into an even greater influence.

Teaching and Scripture reference:

Just Do It!

Hey – that's been my scripture many times!

TO SUM IT UP ...

NOTES TO SELF...

SORRY – you don't have the best Pastor...
...WE DO!

It is without a doubt one of the greatest gifts from God to be placed under the leadership of Pastor Matthew Barnett! Pastor Matthew and Caroline Barnett are truly the greatest Pastors that anyone could ever hope and pray for; and I mean that with all of my heart.

It is so easy to serve in the position of Worship Pastor for Pastor Matthew, the Dream Center and Angelus Temple. A day never goes by without our family giving thanks for the Lord allowing us the honor of serving him, though our Pastors.

You see, here's why it's so cool!

- Pastor Matthew is not one of these Pastors who stays in the back room somewhere during worship and then makes his grand entrance on the last song.

- Pastor Matthew is not one of these Pastors who reads his sermon notes during the worship.

- Pastor Matthew is not one of those Pastors who really doesn't care about how the worship time goes and just cares about the sermon portion of the service.

- Pastor Matthew is not one of those Pastors who wouldn't know a good note from a bad one.

- Pastor Matthew is not one of these Pastors who is completely unaware of the needs of the community in which they live in and what that has to do with worship.

OH NO – on the Contrary!

PASTOR MATTHEW IS:

- A Pastor who is on the front row from the very beginning of worship, jumping and raising his hands.

- A Pastor who is totally submerged in worship and with the move of God.

- A Pastor who is completely submerged in the pulse and spiritual temperature of that room and service at all times.

- A Pastor who is completely aware of what the Lord has for his congregation and prepares in advance for his sermons as well as every part of that service.

- A Pastor who <u>can't</u> dance, sing or play ☺ – but is as much in tune and aware of every note, word, melody and phrase as I am.

- A Pastor who spends time seeking the Lord for the next fresh move of worship for our church.

- A Pastor who is remarkably aware of the community around him and the needs of everyone he meets; and he uses every part of every service to reach the lost and hurting people!

Be sure to pray and thank the Lord for your Pastor everyday! You may only have SECOND best – but you are blessed with individuals who have committed their lives to loving and helping people. Look for every way you can to be a support and blessing to them in return!

Your worship team should …

be your Pastor's biggest FAN CLUB!

TO SUM IT UP ...

PMB is our biggest FAN...
and we are HIS!

NOTES TO SELF...